Test It!

by Abbie Rushton
illustrated by Farimah Khavarinezhad

AF584142

OXFORD
UNIVERSITY PRESS

Lin likes testing things.

Have an adult near to help!

Will It Fizz?

Put a coin in the pop.

Put a mint in the pop.

Will It Sink?

What will sink down?

This is a foil boat.
Add coins to it.
Will it sink?

Oil Art

You will need ...

oil
food ink
a dropper

1. Fill the glasses from the tap.

2. Add 4 drops of ink.

3. Mix the ink.

4. Put oil in the dish.

5. Add drops to the dish of oil.

Can You Hear?

You will need ...

Get the string.

Put cups on the ends of the string.

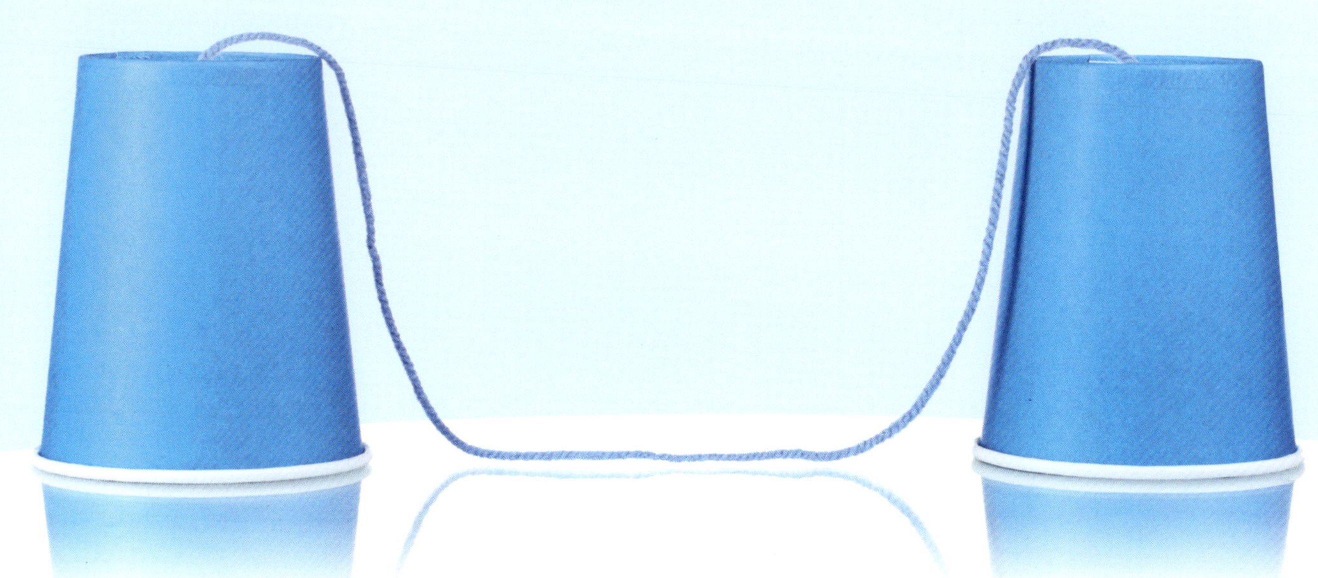

Pull the string tight.

The tests were so good!
You can have a go now. Test it!

What will sink?
Have a think, then test it!

pen

spoon

twig

bricks

Encourage students to consider whether the items will sink or float. If appropriate, allow them to test it.